S0-AXM-070

Camel or sable hair mop (quill)

Camel, sable or bear hair mop

Pencil brush

Hog hair fitch

Brush for staining

BRUSHES USED IN FRENCH POLISHING

THE FRENCH POLISHER'S MANUAL

A DESCRIPTION OF FRENCH POLISHING METHODS AND TECHNIQUE

WITH ILLUSTRATIONS

SECOND EDITION
REVISED AND ENLARGED

London
E. & F. N. SPON LTD.
57, Haymarket, S.W.1
1946

Manufactured in the United States of America

Woodcraft Supply Corporation
313 Montvale Avenue
Woburn, Massachusetts 01801
1978
ISBN 0 - 918036 - 05 - 4

FOREWORD

This Manual was first published more than half a century ago, and it has frequently been reprinted. This new and fully revised edition has been undertaken in order to meet the continued demand for a small handbook on the subject. New methods have been introduced and the old chapters re-written so as to bring them into line with modern practice. Illustrations of the principal items of a French Polisher's equipment have been added.

CONTENTS

ILLUSTRATIONS

Introduction

French polishing is both an art and a craft and it is the purpose of this manual to give the reader whether professional or amateur, a description of the various methods normally employed by successful workers. It must be appreciated, however, that in a book of this size it is not possible to cover the whole field of operations but, nevertheless, by a careful study of its contents, the reader will be able to acquire more than an elementary knowledge of the subject.

It must be emphasized that mastery of the art is dependent not only on a knowledge of the subject but also on the acquisition of that necessary manual dexterity which can best be obtained by perseverance and practice.

The process of French polishing was originally developed in France as a speedier alternative to the older and rather tedious practice of obtaining a polished surface by repeated applications of oils and bees-wax. During the inter-war years the increased demand for polished goods led to the development of the polishing machine, through which the process has lost much of its artistic quality. Mechanization made a further advance with the introduction of cellulose applied by the spraying machine. These newer processes have their specific merits, chief of which is the ease and cheapness with which they can be applied to large-scale production. The peculiar charm of the original French polish, however, remains and is sufficient to ensure its survival in work of the very highest quality.

This manual is intended primarily to appeal to those who wish to practise French polishing as a hand-craft, but some details of the modern mechanical processes have been given, as they call for some modification of the normal polishing procedure, when renovation or re-polishing is contemplated.

Chapter 1

Materials and Equipment

While it is possible for superlative skill to produce, on occasion, a satisfactory result with make-shift appliances, the many practical difficulties will be appreciably diminished by taking advantage of the cumulative experience which has been handed down with the art. A description is given of a typical workshop and the various tools and equipment which the polisher may require. While it is not possible always to achieve this in every detail, some attempt should be made by the polisher to approximate as closely as possible to this ideal.

THE WORKSHOP

The workshop should be as roomy as possible and chosen for its light. Large windows facing to the north are preferable, the north light being more nearly constant and permitting of greater accuracy in colouring and matching. Further, there is the advantage that the direct rays of the sun are excluded, so obviating the creation of misleading tones in the colour of the work. Fog, frost and damp are conducive to " chilled " polish and, in view of the fact that these conditions are more often encountered near ground level, it is an advantage to locate the workshop on an upper floor.

Of all decorative schemes, white reflects the most light and introduces no alien tones and it should, therefore, be adopted for walls and ceiling. Artificial lighting should be so arranged as to prevent undue shadow effects and should be approximately of daylight intensity. No artificial light ordinarily obtainable, is truly comparable to daylight and the polisher would be well advised not to attempt to colour or to match in such a light if it could be avoided.

An even temperature of approximately 60 degrees F. should, as far as possible, be maintained in the workshop and, bearing in mind that dust is one of the worst enemies of the French polisher, every effort to achieve a dust-free atmosphere should be made.

Ample cupboard room should be provided for the storing of stock for use. Open shelves have the great disadvantage as against enclosed cupboards in that the dust tends to collect freely on the miscellaneous array of bottles, which normally forms such a large part of the polisher's stock-in-trade, and this can be removed only with some difficulty and waste of valuable time.

A gas ring, or some similar source of heat, should be installed for the purpose of making up stains.

THE BENCH

Fig. 1 illustrates a suitable bench which may vary in size between 2′ 6″ and 3′ in width and between 5′ and 6′ in length. Preferably it should not be a fixture but built up on trestles, as this form of construction is essentially portable and will enable the operator to dismantle it or adjust its position at will, in order to obtain the utmost advantage from the available light.

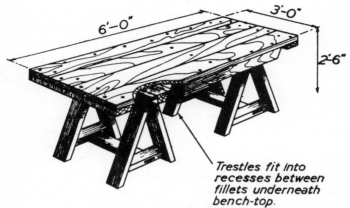

6'-0"   3'-0"   2'-6"

*Trestles fit into
recesses between
fillets underneath
bench-top.*

Fig. 1—Typical French Polisher's Bench

BRUSHES AND MISCELLANEOUS ITEMS

The polisher should familiarize himself at the outse t with the various items of his equipment which will con - sist of a selection of brushes of various types; rags; wad - ding; canvas; glass-paper (Nos. oo, o, 1, 1½ and fine 2) emery powder; pumice powder; bees-wax; plaster of Paris; sugar soap; household soda; oxalic acid; a few cabinet maker's tools such as screwdriver, hammer, pliers, chisel and scraper; a selection of tins, pots, pails and bottles; broom and dusters. A few "bench-pads" measuring be- tween 2' and 3' (see Fig. 2) made of wooden slats and covered with green baize will be a convenience, if not a necessity, to support finished work without damage to the polished surface.

The Frontispiece illustrates some of the brushes which are normally to be found in a polisher's equipment. These consist of mops in camel- sable- and bear-hair in various sizes, a decorator's grass distemper brush, a painter's sash tool, and a few domestic flat-backed brushes, such as a boot-brush and nail-brush. Each of these has its specific use which will be fully explained when dealing with the appropriate process.

POLISHES AND VARNISHES

The principal items of the polisher's stock-in-trade are French polishes of various kinds, stains and solvents. French polish is a generic term which is applied to a variety of polishes all of which have, as basic constituents, shellac dissolved in methylated spirit. These two ingredients form a pure polish to which a small proportion of such gums as sandarac, mastic, benzoin and tragacanth are invariably added in order to hasten the hardening process or to give an improved lustre to the finished work. The shellac used may be either in its natural state or bleached, the latter being used when a relatively transparent or colourless polish is required. While these ingredients can be obtained by those who wish to make up their own polishes, a good quality polish ready for use can be obtained from any reputable polish and varnish manufacturer and this course is ordinarily to be preferred. The varieties most commonly used are dark polish, garnet polish, button polish, white polish, transparent polish, orange (or brown) polish, black polish and glaze.

Varnishes, while not strictly speaking to be included in a work on French polishing, are frequently required by the polisher for such special purposes as the touching up of faulty spots on carvings, etc. In general, they are more viscous and "gummy" than polishes, but have a similarity in that both polish and varnish consist of a gum dissolved in a suitable solvent. The most common varnishes used by the polisher are brown hard varnish, naphtha varnish, white hard varnish, copal varnish and china varnish.

STAINS, SOLVENTS AND POWDERED COLOURS

The operation of staining resembles painting so closely that the basic difference between the two processes often remains unnoticed. In painting, a change of colour is secured by depositing on the surface a film consisting of minute coloured particles which, to a greater or lesser extent, obscure the wood beneath them. This is more likely to be an advantage than a disadvantage where common timber is concerned, and graining, a derivative of painting, was developed to suggest artificially a figuring which the original timber did not possess. The French polisher, however, works almost exclusively on the choicer woods, where the figuring is often its especial charm. Here, staining, which consists in actually colouring the wood to some small depth, not only preserves the original figuring but, by the selective absorption of the stain by the wood, heightens the contrast and enhances its beauty, while at the same time changing the colour to one either more agreeable or more in keeping with the design or purpose of the article.

Stains are classified in three main groups according to the vehicle used—water, oil or spirit. They are further divisible into those producing a change of colour by direct chemical action, those which dye the wood, and the more or less insoluble pigments which rely for their effect upon a film of coloured particles on the surface of the wood.

The chief drawbacks to water stain are that it has a tendency to raise and roughen the grain of the wood and that it also takes longer to dry. It is, however, regarded as

being the best stain for general use since, besides being
cheaper, it has a greater degree of transparency than the
other types and is also more permanent. Both oil and
spirit stains raise the grain less, but tend to fade, and oil
stain has the further disadvantages that it reflects a rather
dull and "gloomy" background, takes longer to dry, and
may cause the work to sweat subsequently.

Most water and spirit stains can be purchased in powder or crystal form, ready for dilution by the user to the
required strength, and ordinarily this course is recommended to the beginner. Should he prefer to mix his own,
however, he will find the powdered aniline dyes very
suitable for his purpose. They are normally manufactured to be either water-soluble or spirit-soluble and care
should be taken to specify which kind is required.

Spirit stains tend to give a more powerful result than
water stains and are popular in view of their drying so
quickly, a property which does much to reduce the time
between successive operations. Where large areas are
concerned, this rapid evaporation of the spirit can become
a disadvantage, as owing to the higher cost of spirit
stains, there is a tendency (for the sake of economy) to
make them up in reduced quantities and to apply them
with a smaller brush, all of which makes an even application more difficult. Where work is to be renovated or
repolished, the spirit stain is useful in that it will "take"
over places where sufficient of the old polish remains to
have "proofed" the part against the action of a water
stain.

Bichromate of potash in aqueous solution is not a stain
in the strict sense of the term, as the wood is coloured by
chemical action between the solution and itself. The
wood being a contributory factor towards the resulting
colour, the use of this chemical is limited to mahogany

and oak, a strong solution applied to the latter producing the popular Golden Oak colour. Bichromate has no appreciable effect on other woods.

Permanganate of potash, when used in a strong aqueous solution, forms a very cheap brown chemical stain. It is hardly to be recommended, however, as it fades rather quickly in some conditions and does not produce an even colour. It also attacks the hair in the brushes used for staining and should be applied with either a grass brush or cotton swab.

Powdered pigments, whether dry or ground in water or oil, are not truly soluble in either medium and consequently interpose a coloured film between the wood and the polish. Added to the polish, the dry powders are extremely useful for matching and securing special colour effects. In the making of water stain either the powder or the colours ground in water may be used, but in the preparation of oil stain it is more convenient to use them ready ground in oil. These pigments are, practically speaking, permanent.

Varnish stains, as their name suggests, are a mixture of varnish and stain and, as such, fall definitely within the paint class. At best, they involve the operator in the physical difficulty of so applying them as to secure a full varnished appearance without, at the same time, totally obscuring the wood by the stain. They are not to be recommended and, their use being restricted to giving a quick and convenient finish to the cheapest work, they have little or no importance for the French polisher.

FILLERS

Unless the work is to be left open-grained, as is usual in the case of oak, it will be necessary for the polisher to fill up the tiny indentations of the grain. Plaster of Paris is often used for this purpose and has the merit of cheapness. Proprietary brands of specially prepared wood fillers of appropriate colours are now obtainable and, in so far as they resist more successfully the tendency of subsequent glass-papering to dislodge them, they are more effective in use.

Chapter 2

French Polishing Stage by Stage

PREPARATION

French polishing, reduced to its simplest terms, consists in covering the surface of the wood with a perfectly smooth film of shellac. The very simplicity of the definition hides the practical difficulties which the performer only too readily discovers for himself, unless he has the patience to execute each stage of the process thoroughly and without hurry. When it is realised that the film of polish which is to adhere to the wood is only a few thousandths of an inch in thickness, it will be obvious that, if this final surface is to be smooth, that of the wood immediately beneath must be equally so, before any of the polishing operations can be commenced.

It is assumed that the work has already been "finished". This means that any nails or sprigs should have been sunk beneath the surface with a punch, that glue stains should have been removed and the whole work cleaned up with a keen, finely adjusted smoothing plane. Faint ridges from the plane iron are likely still to persist in the surface and, although invisible at this stage, will reappear, even after glass-papering, in an unpleasantly exaggerated form when the work is finally polished. After planing, therefore, the work should be well scraped with

a cabinet maker's steel scraper before rubbing down with
fine glass-paper wrapped round a flat cork block and
applied in the direction of the grain. Where there is
cross-banding or finely figured curls or burrs, a circular
motion should be used.

These operations, if carefully carried out, will have
done a great deal towards the achievement of a smooth
surface, but two further sources of imperfection remain,
the first being the small fissures of the grain itself, and
the second the potentiality of the fibres of the wood for
swelling and "raising the grain" when wetted by the
various solutions used in the succeeding operations. It is
most convenient to counteract this latter defect at this
stage and for this reason the cabinet maker "damps
down" his work with hot water and puts it aside to dry.
This application of water has the effect of swelling or
raising the grain, which can then be levelled again with
the finest grade of glass-paper over a cork block and
working in the direction of the grain. The work should
now be dusted down carefully and, to simplify the subsequent operations, all removable parts, such as doors and
mouldings, should be taken off. To ensure that all parts
may eventually be reassembled in the correct positions,
the polisher should mark both the part and the position it
occupied with corresponding Roman numerals which can
conveniently be indented by means of a screwdriver. The
operator must, of course, take care to mark only those
surfaces which will be concealed on reassembly.

It is axiomatic to say that the various faults are the
more perfectly concealed the earlier in the process they
are corrected. For this reason the polisher should now
examine the article thoroughly. Any small holes or ill-
fitting joints should be "stopped" with hard stopping or
plastic wood. Both these preparations are sold in several

shades and it is generally more convenient to purchase them ready made. It must be borne in mind that the stain does not "take" on this stopping, so that it is essential that the stopping should be chosen to match the finished work. Dents, bruises and scratches, if they are slight and the wood not too hard, may be removed by applying a little hot water and, when dry, glass-papering over the spot. More stubborn cases may be corrected by placing a rag soaked in water over the spot and applying a hot iron. If the part is veneered, it must be remembered that the veneer is held in place by glue and is likely to be detached or blistered as a result of the water and heat, and the polisher should, therefore, proceed very cautiously. Any scratches or bruises too deep to be removed in this way must be treated like holes and filled with hard stopping of appropriate colour. Should the work have received water splashes in carrying out these or previous operations, it should be dried and glass-papered thoroughly, as otherwise the splashes will tend to be unduly absorbent to stain and will appear darker in the finished work.

Should the work have been inlaid or ornamented with stringings or bandings, it will be necessary to prevent their being discoloured in the subsequent staining operation. If water stain is to be used, this can be effected quite simply by painting carefully over those portions to be protected, two or three times with white polish, using a pencil camel-hair brush. Great care must be observed not to allow the polish to flow over the surrounding wood.

Unless the whole work has been fabricated of wood taken from the same tree, or carefully selected, it is almost certain that some variation in colour will exist at the commencement. When the article is to be finished in a dark colour this inequality can be rectified in the staining operation, but when the finish is to be light or "natural" it will be necessary to bleach the darker portions with an oxalic acid solution made by dissolving two ounces of oxalic acid in one pint of hot water. This acid is poisonous and should be used with care and applied with a small rag mop. After drying, the oxalic acid should be "killed" by washing the work down with vinegar.

The article should now be ready for staining.

STAINING

In view of their general convenience, it is assumed that a ready-made variety of water or spirit stain is to be used. The required colour should be obtained and made up in accordance with the directions. It is a point always to be borne in mind that, whereas it is a simple matter to deepen a stain that is too light, it is not so easy to wash off a deposit that is heavier than desired. Furthermore, the washing has a tendency to produce a dull effect, lacking in the brilliance to be obtained by two weaker stainings. The polisher should therefore be cautious and test the stain for strength on a small strip of wood, or on a hidden piece of the work, before application.

The beginner is recommended to use a water stain at the outset, as a larger brush may be used and he will appreciate the benefit of not having to hurry the operation unduly. A grass brush, similar to the decorator's distemper brush (see Frontispiece), is a very useful tool and the stain should be applied in full, flowing coats, both across and in the direction of the grain, to ensure that the stain is absorbed into the grain. The polisher should take particular care not to miss crevices or corners or the "quirks" of the mouldings. The stain should then be wiped off with a rag in the direction of the grain, taking care that no streaks or runs are left on the work. It is as well to realize that the depth of the staining depends to a considerable extent on the time during which the stain is left soaking into the wood, and the interval between application and wiping off should, by following the same sequence, be maintained as constant as possible. In the case of a large surface, too large an area should not be stained at one time before it is wiped dry as, otherwise, variations are likely to be revealed afterwards. The work should be placed aside to dry thoroughly.

When the first application of stain is dry, the polisher must decide whether the work is dark enough and whether the colouring is uniform. The appearance of the work at this moment will be flat and dull and it is a matter of difficulty, and needs considerable experience, to visualize the finished appearance with certainty. The beginner may simulate the effect of the finished polish for a few moments, by wiping the article with a rag soaked in methylated spirit. Should a second staining be considered necessary, it is generally more convenient to do this by means of a rag soaked in the stain, as the operation can thus be performed with greater discrimination and the stain applied only to those parts which require darkening. The work should again be set aside to dry thoroughly.

The above outline of the staining operation applies, with suitable variation in the choice of the stain, to all timbers, but mahogany may, if preferred, be stained with a chemical stain made by dissolving bichromate of potash crystals in water. Here again the strength of the stain should be tested on a trial piece of the wood. Oak and walnut, when required in a dark shade, may be coloured with a stain composed of vandyke crystals dissolved in water to which an alkali in the form of washing soda or ammonia has been added (half an ounce of ammonia to one pint of water). A mixture of bichromate of potash and vandyke crystals is effective for oak and walnut where a golden tone is required. In dealing with natural coloured walnut articles which may, for structural reasons, contain certain parts made of birch or beech, the grey effect needed can be obtained with a very weak stain of copperas in water.

Years ago, it was discovered that oak, when used in stables, assumed a dark colour, which we now recognise as "fumed" oak. The discolouration was found to be caused by the presence of ammonia fumes and the effect is now obtained by enclosing the oak in a room or box with trays of ammonia solution. For large work, a small room or specially constructed cabinet, which must be reasonably gas-tight to prevent the escape of the fumes, is used. For small work a plywood tea-chest will be found very useful or, failing this, the work may be treated directly by applying the ammonia solution with a brush. The fumes make this latter operation difficult and the results are not quite so satisfactory as those obtained by the purely fume method.

FILLING IN

The polisher must now decide whether he prefers to polish his work "open grain" or, by filling up the pores of the grain, ultimately deliver an article with a perfectly smooth and glass-like surface. This latter finish is referred to as polishing "full grain" and is that normally used in polishing mahogany, walnut and most other woods. Oak is generally polished open grain as the full grain finish is not considered to be in keeping with its somewhat rugged characteristics, but an exception is made in the case of straw-coloured oak which appears to greater effect when polished full grain.

The earliest French polishers achieved their full grain effects by choking up the grain with shellac polish alone. The process was somewhat tedious, as repeated applications were necessary, each of which had to be set aside to harden before rubbing, or "cutting", down with glass-paper or powdered pumice. In so far as the grain was built up on the sure foundation of layers of thoroughly and individually hardened polish, it could be expected to have some claims to permanence. In fact, some of the work of these early polishers still possesses a lustrous smoothness which has probably never been surpassed, and for this reason this procedure is still adopted for work of the very highest quality.

Development and progress, as is so often the case, have been directed towards greater output in less time and the modern methods of filling in the grain depend upon choking the pores with various plastic mixtures which solidify and, after glass-papering, leave a perfectly level surface upon which subsequent coatings of polish may be deposited. As this operation has now become a part of the normal polishing technique, it is proposed to explain it in detail.

After the work has dried naturally and thoroughly, following the staining operation, it should be very lightly glass-papered using a piece of well-worn fine glass-paper over a flat cork block. Great care must be taken not to cut through the stain and so produce lighter areas which, in subsequent operations, will be found difficult to obliterate, the edges being specially dangerous in this respect. The work should then be "stopped" by coating it all over quickly and evenly with button polish applied either with a gilder's mop or, alternatively, with a fad—

a fad (see Fig. 4) being an old polish rubber which has already fulfilled its period of usefulness in its original capacity. A new polishing rubber must on no account be used, as whiskers of wadding will inevitably fasten themselves to the surface. The purpose of stopping the work is primarily to prevent any possibility of the filler discolouring it, but it also helps towards the production of a transparent quality in the final result. It is, furthermore, an additional safeguard against the possibilities of subsequent sweating.

After stopping the work, it must be lightly glass-papered again to remove dust specks and any small nibs which may have adhered to the surface as a result of the application of the polish. The article is now ready for filling in.

If a proprietary brand of wood filler is purchased, it should be thinned down in accordance with the manufacturer's directions and brushed on to the work as if it were paint, the objective being to work it well into the grain. The work is then allowed to stand until the filler has set sufficiently to allow of the surplus being wiped off with a piece of coarse hessian or canvas rubbed across the grain, without at the same time removing the filler from the small fissures and so defeating the object of the operation. For this same reason the wiping off should never be performed in the direction of the grain.

A home-made filler can be prepared by mixing plaster of Paris with a suitable dry powdered colour and forming the mixture into a stiff paste by the addition of white oil (three parts) and button polish (one part). Linseed oil may be used in place of the white oil, but there is an attendant risk in the indiscriminate use of linseed oil in the early stages, in that it may be absorbed into the wood and so become imprisoned under the subsequent layers of polish, thence eventually to succeed in finding an outlet by oozing through the finished surface. This defect is known as "sweating" and is best avoided by a sparing use of linseed oil throughout the various stages.

The filler should be applied to the surface with a brisk, circular motion by means of a piece of canvas upon which a liberal coating of the preparation has been smeared. Any surplus should be wiped off, care always being taken to work across the grain. The presence of polish in the filler is conducive to rapid hardening and the polisher should not, therefore, fill in so much at a time as to cause difficulty for himself in the wiping-off operation. Mouldings and crevices which are difficult to wipe clean, may be cleaned out with a slip of wood of approximately pencil thickness, one end of which has been sharpened to a point and the other to a chisel edge. Carvings are not normally filled in and any filler which has inadvertently found its way to such portions of the work should be brushed out as soon as possible with a nail-brush or some similar stiff-bristled brush.

When the filler has thoroughly dried, the work should again be lightly rubbed down with worn glass-paper and then carefully dusted down. Another brush coating of polish should now be given and, if the work is in mahogany, it will be an advantage in the later stages, if this brush coating is tinted very slightly with red polish, although red polish—or dragon's blood as some polishers call it—is now rarely used. In the case of other woods, either button polish, garnet polish, or dark French polish should be used, according to the tone required.

The filling-in process, as outlined above, applies to all woods, the only modification necessary being in the colouring matter added. Although the operator will gain from experience a knowledge of the colours needed and the amounts required, the following suggested colours may be of assistance at the commencement:

Satinwood Satin Walnut Ash Elm *Birch *Beech	} Yellow ochre
Walnut Teak Dark Oak (usually left open grained)	} Burnt or raw umber
Mahogany	Rose Pink or Purple Brown
Rosewood	Rose Pink with a small addition of Gas Black
Ebony	Gas or Vegetable Black.

*Where items of birch or beech form part of an article in walnut or mahogany, they should be coloured to match the main timber.

FADDING-IN

The previous operations may be classed strictly as preparatory ones but, with the process known as "fadding-in", or "sizing-in", the polisher makes a beginning on the first of the real polishing stages.

After the brush coating of polish which concludes the filling-in, the surface of the wood will be in a semi-absorbent state and it will probably not have escaped the eye of the observant worker that the polish tends to soak into some parts of the work more readily than others. No further advance can be made towards the ultimate objective of a rich, even polish until all porous parts have been saturated sufficiently for the surface to have become uniform and, what is more important, to have achieved some stability. From the point of view of quality alone, nothing has been found superior for this purpose to repeated applications of polish, applied with a polishing rubber and worked well into the grain, with frequent intervals during which the work is set aside and allowed to harden. Hurriedly polished work, in the execution of which hardening time has been curtailed in an effort to achieve quick results, consists of a polished surface which, as one of the inevitable effects of time, will, to some extent, contract and sink into the grain, destroying in its progress the finish of the surface. The French polisher must, therefore, keep constantly in mind the fact that careful groundwork in the early stages, plus unhurried work in the polishing stages, are most conducive to a perfect and permanent finish.

With these first applications of polish, the main tool will become the rubber which, briefly, is a pad of cotton wool more or less saturated with polish. This pad is covered with a lintless cotton or linen rag which has been previously well washed to remove all traces of dressing and lime. This rag covering serves, to some extent, as a filter for the polish by preventing the transference of any solid impurities to the work. It further presents a durable surface to withstand the considerable friction subsequently to be developed when polishing is in progress.

The polisher will find it useful to have rubbers of several sizes; these, when not in use, should be kept in an air-tight tin until again required for, if left about to dry out, which they very quickly do, they become quite unusable. If the period of idleness is likely to be prolonged, a piece of cotton wool soaked in methylated spirit and placed at the botton of the tin, will serve to preserve them almost indefinitely.

A useful size of polishing rubber can be made by taking a piece of cotton wadding measuring approximately 6″ x 5″ (medicated cotton wool which, from the polisher's point of view, contains impurities, should on no account be used). After removal of the thin protective film, the wadding may be moulded into a pad similar in shape to a pear (see Fig. 5) and must now be charged with polish. A wine or vinegar bottle is a useful container for the polish. A convenient method of controlling the contents, which, at the same time, mitigates the effects of accidentally knocking over the bottle, is afforded by cutting a vee groove in the side of the cork so that the polish is discharged in a steady trickle. In the case of a new rubber, the face should be anointed with approximately a dessertspoonful of polish which should be allowed to soak into the wadding as it trickles from the bottle. At the beginning the rubber tends to discharge its polish rather freely and it is safer to err on the side of caution, at least until the polisher has some familiarity with the process. When the rubber is being charged or re-charged, it should be noted that the wrapping must first be removed and the applications of polish made direct to the wadding.

The polisher should now take a piece of linen or calico, measuring approximately 9″ x 7″, into the centre of which he should place the wadding, charged side downwards. The rag should then be folded round the pad (see Figs. 6 and 7), care being taken to mould it so that the pear-like appearance is maintained. Any surplus rag should be worked and twisted up to the back of the pad, the polisher bearing in mind that it is of paramount importance that the working face of the finished pad should be perfectly free from creases or wrinkles and should remain so under all conditions of polishing. To complete the moulding of the rubber it is a good plan to press its face on to the back of a piece of used glass-paper or clean piece of wood, so that the face is flat and slightly pointed towards the tip, rather like a flat-iron. In use, the rubber should be held firmly in the palm of the hand (see Fig. 8), the back of the rubber, with the surplus rag twisted round it, forming a ball-like pad which will gradually mould itself with use, to the shape of the hand. Fingers and thumb should firmly grip the sides of the rubber, the forefinger being placed on the point, this part being particularly useful when recessed panels with carvings are being worked.

With the rubber charged ready for use, the fadding-in can be started by working up and down the surface lightly in the direction of the grain. Too much pressure should not be used at first as a new rubber tends to discharge its polish somewhat freely. The beginner should avoid traversing the same portion again without leaving an interval for the polish to harden, but unless the work is very small, it is normally sufficient merely to cover the work in strict sequence. As the work progresses, it will be found that pressure may be increased and that the amount of polish deposited can be suitably controlled by the squeezing action of the fingers on the rubber. The wood will be absorbent and it will be found that the rubber must be replenished frequently. One of the objects of the fadding-in is to prepare a skin of polish on the wood which will prevent any oil used subsequently from penetrating the wood, and, for this reason, oil must not be used at this stage, though, in any case, the fad should be found to work quite freely without its assistance.

The polisher will now gradually gather some impression of the likely appearance of the work when finished and he may notice holes and scratches which will need attention. These should be filled up with coloured wax or hard stopping made from melted bees-wax or paraffin wax to which an appropriate powdered colour has been added. A pen-knife is a suitable tool with which to force the wax into the apertures, any surplus being removed by rubbing with the back or smooth surface of a piece of glass-paper; this, without interfering with the surface of the wood, will reduce the wax to the level of the work. The fadding should then be continued until the work shows signs of the growing stickiness, which, throughout all the polishing operations, is the danger signal to the novice. He should immediately place the work aside to harden for an hour or two or, preferably, leave it over-night. On resuming work, the article should be very lightly glass-papered and can then be bodied-in with polish slightly diluted with methylated spirit. The rubber, after being charged with this diluted polish, should be worked in circular, oval and figure-of-eight paths as illustrated in Figs. 9, 10, 11 and 12. At this stage a mere touch of raw linseed oil on the surface of the rubber will lubricate it and prevent it dragging the polish. The minimum possible quantity should be used and it is sufficient to invert the linseed oil bottle and dab its wetted cork on the surface of the rubber. The purpose of the circular motions in using the rubber is to force polish well into the grain and, by changing the pattern, to ensure that the deposit is even throughout. The oil smears left on the surface will afford some indication that the motions of the rubber are overlapping correctly, and the covering of the work rhythmically in this manner auto-matically ensures that each part will have an interval in which to harden, before it is again subjected to the action of the rubber. This is of material assistance in preventing the work from becoming gummy and dragging on the rubber, a condition which so frequently preludes disaster for the novice.

When the work appears to have become too soft to proceed further, it should be placed aside to harden.

Before leaving the fadding stage, some mention must be made of the special methods which must be adopted in dealing with such irregularities as frets, carvings and mouldings, where the normal polishing rubber cannot be employed. The richness of carvings and frets is considerably enhanced if, by way of contrast, these portions are left semi-polished, so giving the appearance of a waxed finish. This effect is secured by jiggering the work out with a painter's fitch and using polish diluted with an equal volume of methylated spirit. Mouldings should be worked with a relatively dry fad which, with practice, can be made to shape itself to the exact contour of the moulding. The operator must, however, be careful to ensure that it makes contact with the recesses or quirks as otherwise these portions will not receive their full deposits of polish.

COLOURING OR MATCHING

During the final stages of the preceding operation the polisher will have been able to estimate fairly accurately the probable appearance of the finished article. It is certain that, unless the work has been fashioned from timber taken from a single tree and great care taken to stain it evenly, some portions will show considerable variations in colour. Further, it may be that the article appears, in general, somewhat lighter than other items of furniture with which it is to be associated and, for this reason, it may be necessary to darken it to prevent an odd appearance. In any case, it can be said that, for one reason or another, practically every job will require some form of colour adjustment which is more easily effected at this stage, when an accurate impression of the final appearance can be obtained and there is still no heavy deposit of polish to make a transparent effect difficult of attainment. There is the further advantage that subsequent layers of polish will be a protection against fading.

The degree to which uniformity of colour throughout a piece of work must be secured is a matter of some controversy. While it is obvious and beyond argument that variations of colour so acute as to produce a definitely odd effect are to be avoided, a good case can be made for retaining some of the slight variations in colour which may be said to be part of the character of the wood. In some respects the modern cabinets made from plastics supply a useful illustration of the synthetic monotony and mechanistic effect of extreme colour uniformity. In any event, whether the polisher believes in reducing all colour variations to a minimum or in controlling them to secure a definite artistic effect, it is a matter which must rest entirely upon his own discretion and the degree of his artistic skill. The possibilities of control, at this stage, are so great that the unwary beginner is likely to be carried away by enthusiasm into a demonstration of his power to change the colour of the whole work: It is, however, very easy to destroy the careful work of early stages and it is wiser to err on the side of under-colouring. "When in doubt, don't!" forms a very useful guide in this matter.

It must be realised that the colour of an object is modified by the colour of the light by which it is illuminated and, for this reason, the polisher is advised never to attempt to colour an article by artificial light. If the matching consists in the mere evening-up of colour variations in the article itself, it will be sufficient if the job is reassembled and stood facing the window, but should it be necessary to adjust the colour to match that of some other piece of furniture, it is preferable for the matching to be done in the actual room and position the piece will eventually occupy. This is, of course, in some respects a counsel of perfection and no doubt the polisher in practice must be content with placing his work in front of the window and with holding the pattern as close to it as possible. In any case, he should take the precaution of keeping the pattern the right way up so as to reduce the possibility of error. He must also, when making this comparison, allow for the darkening effect of subsequent applications of polish.

The colour of the work may vary in two ways—in "shade" and in "tone". The term "shade" is related to the density of a specific colour and may be visualized by considering the variation which takes place when either more water or more dye is added in the preparation of a water-stain. "Tone" refers to a modification of the colour itself as occurs, for instance, when yellow is added to a red or a blue to the same red. It will be obvious after consideration of these definitions that, given a stain of a tone correct to match the darker portions of the work, variations in the shade elsewhere can be corrected by the application of a number of diluted coatings of that stain. This forms the theoretical basis of successful practical colouring.

At the conclusion of fadding-in, the work will have been left with a thin and hardened film of polish over its surface and it will be obvious, even to the novice with his slight experience, that neither water stain nor oil stain can be effectively used, as such stains will not "take" on the polish. It is necessary, therefore, to have recourse to a modified spirit stain which consists of an appropriate dye or colour in a mixture of methylated spirit (two parts) and polish (one part). The spirit basis of this stain allows it to bite into the existing surface and the proportion of polish serves to act as a binder for those colours which are not truly soluble in the spirit. The polisher must realise that the wood has now lost that selective absorbency which was so instrumental in enhancing its natural beauty and figuring during the staining operation and that, in place of this, the film of shellac deposited while fadding-in, has rendered it sensibly uniform in its ability to soak up spirit stain. This is obvious to the experienced polisher; it is laboured here as a warning to the beginner against a heavy application of stain which will have the effect of obliterating, or partially obscuring, the beauty of the grain which he has, up to now, been at such pains to preserve.

Where an article is found to be wholly lighter than the pattern, a convenient way of making the necessary adjustment is to work over it with several rubbers of polish to which a suitable colour has been added. The colou should not be strong and when sufficient modification has been achieved the operator should revert to polishing with a stain-free rubber. Where considerable variations of colour exist throughout a piece of work and it is desired to achieve some uniformity, the usual process consists of darkening the light parts until they are comparable with the rest. This is effected by the use of spirit stain applied either with a camel-hair mop or, as some experienced workers prefer, with a rubber, the latter

Fig. 2.—BENCH PAD

Fig. 3.—THE BENZER

Fig. 4—THE FAD

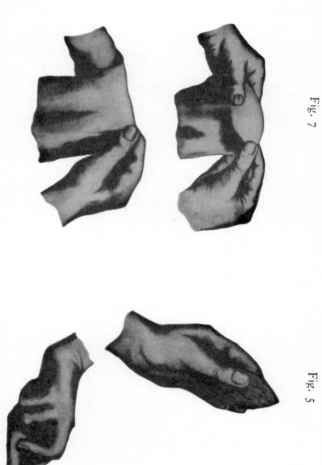

Fig. 7

Fig. 5

Fig. 6

Fig. 8

FOLDING THE RUBBER

method tending to give a more even result on the larger areas.

The stain is made by enclosing suitable colours in a small bag made of two or three thicknesses of rag, the whole being agitated and squeezed, dolly-tint fashion, in the mixture of polish and spirit. The rag acts as a filter and prevents any small solid particles from being incorporated in the stain and eventually finding their way on to the work. The bag should be removed when the required colour, as ascertained by a test, has been secured. This colour should approximate to the darker portions of the work as regards tone and should be a shade or so lighter. In colouring with a mop, the mop should be squeezed between the forefinger and the edge of the jar so that it is wet but not dripping. It should then be applied to the work rapidly, in the direction of the grain, from end to end of the work, without pause, in a flowing coat. The next stroke should be applied in the same direction but just slightly overlapping the first. The brush should be kept moist so that the dye is lightly and easily applied but with no tendency to run; if it should do so over an edge it should be wiped away instantly with the finger before it loosens the polish. In view of the fact that the spirit in the stain softens the polished film beneath, it is obvious that the laboured brush work of the painter is inappropriate, and no attempt should be made to go over the work a second time until the surface has again become dry and hard. This should be after half an hour or so and, if the work still appears to be too light, a further application of the stain should be made. On hardening finally, the work should be rubbed down very lightly with well-used No. oo glass-paper, lubricated with a drop of oil, to remove any specks which may have adhered thereto, but it must be remembered that the stain is superficial and care must be taken not to apply the glass-paper so vigorously as to cause a patchy effect. The work should now be dusted down and given a brush coating of polish applied with a clean mop, which may conveniently be the mop used for staining, if this has been well rinsed in methylated spirit.

The foregoing paragraphs are a summary of all that need be known in the actual application of the stain, but it remains for the polisher to acquire, with practice, the necessary dexterity. At the beginning he may have difficulty in regard to the choice of the stain required to achieve the desired colour adjustment and the following list of colours may form a helpful working basis, which he will be able to modify later in the light of experience and of the needs of a particular article.

Mahogany.—Bismark brown and a little aniline black or gas black will, with the addition of a little red polish, cover most requirements, although it must be realised that the use of these dyes will tend to obscure the grain and to produce a muddy effect. The polisher is, therefore, advised to use them with caution. The red polish is made up by putting some Bismark brown or red sanders wood into a jar with a little methylated spirit, the resulting solution being strained through a piece of muslin into a bottle containing thick polish. Red sanders wood has an advantage over Bismark brown in the matter of permanence, but it requires a longer period in which to soak and the resultant polish is not so powerful in colour. It is a good plan to have a small jar containing the mixture of Bismark brown, polish and spirit, and a similar one with gas or aniline black, as the colouring ingredients. In any event, it is advisable to make the stain by the straining-bag method, as trouble from small particles of powder is thus minimised, and the finer division of the colouring matter will tend to maintain the transparency and clarity of the colour.

Although these primary dyes are all that the beginner will probably require, the further addition of a small bottle with green aniline and one each of yellow aniline and crysadine will be found useful as the polisher's confidence increases. Where parts of the work have a tendency towards excessive redness, compared with the pattern or the desired colour, they can be "killed" or reduced by the use of a little green aniline or, if this would make them too dark, the yellow aniline can be used in its stead. In a similar fashion, yellow aniline or crysadine can be applied to reduce a part which is a shade or so too dark, but these colours must be used with extreme caution and it is preferable to apply them with a fad.

Walnut.—Where, in a light walnut article, it is necessary to fake component parts of beech or birch, so as to resemble the main woodwork, litharge or other lead colours may be required and should be mixed by the straining method. To secure the best result, it is likely that the faking of these parts may have to be extended to graining them so as to resemble the walnut portions. In this case it is necessary first to produce the background colour or groundwork upon which figuring, in imitation of the choicer wood, is then painted with a rather dry pencil-brush. With experience and some acquired skill, quite good effects can be readily obtained, but it is as well for the figuring to be irregular and of varying shades. To this end, the polisher should study closely the grain of the wood in the main structure and endeavour to copy the figuring as closely as possible.

Any inlay or marquetry should be carefully freed from any colouring which may inadvertently have encroached thereon, gentle scraping with a sharp penknife being all that is required to ensure that only the colour is removed.

Often some patches may require faking, but with experience and common-sense, and an intelligent application of these principles, the polisher will find that they can be dealt with successfully.

VARNISHING

Varnishing is an alternative to the fastening of the stain with a brush coating of polish, as previously described, and white hard or brown hard spirit varnish may be used according to the colour. When varnish is used with the polish, however, there is a tendency for a skin to be formed on the surface rather than in the grain: again, if too much varnish is used, the surface may become brittle and, as a consequence, chip. Very many polishers oppose the use of varnish for this reason, but no ill effects should result if it is applied with care. Varnish is, in fact, to some extent an advantage, in so far as it fastens the colour more satisfactorily and provides a more solid foundation for subsequent work than does a layer of polish.

Varnish should, however, only be used well thinned down with polish, as there is a great risk of the work being spoilt by the formation of thick patches on the surface. A mixture of equal parts of varnish and polish is perfectly satisfactory. This should be applied with a bear-hair mop in the direction of the grain and with care to ensure that there are no runnings from crevices or carvings. It is absolutely essential that only one coat of varnish should be given, as otherwise there is a likelihood that the surface may tear and so present difficulties at a later stage. As an alternative to applying the varnish with a brush, some polishers use a rubber, this being particularly useful for large and flat surfaces.

The whole work should now be set aside for twelve hours and allowed to harden thoroughly.

BODYING

In this operation the polisher's task is to build up a film of polish on the surface of the wood which, although not thick, should completely fill all pores or grain of the wood. The previous operations of filling, fadding and varnishing, will have made their various contributions towards levelling the surface, but, even so, it will be found that the grain will still absorb more polish before being completely filled up. On this operation more than on any of the previous ones, depends the permanence and appearance of the final polish and, if a "grand piano" polish is desired, unhurried thoroughness is indispensable.

After fastening (or varnishing, if that process has been used), the work should be carefully and lightly glasspapered in the direction of the grain. The surface of the work should then be wiped over with a rag, on which has been poured a little linseed oil, in order to kill the inevitable marks of the glass-papering.

Without forgetting first to unwrap the rubber, it should now be charged with polish, refolded, and applied to the surface of the work in the direction of the grain. The small amount of oil already on the work will make it unnecessary to add any to the rubber for these first applications. A small piece of an old rubber should be used to work up the polish on any mouldings that exist, being easily adapted so as to conform to their shape. With a little practice the quirks can be worked up quite cleanly. Carvings are often left jiggered out with thinned down polish to produce a waxed finish, but generally they should be polished more fully, and treated in the same way as mouldings, a dulling brush and pumice powder being used to give a soft effect. Similarly, frets are quite often left with a waxed finish but, if they too are to be fully polished, care must be taken to avoid the polish running or causing tears, and this is best achieved by leaving the polishing of all frets until the rubber has worked itself nearly dry. Normally, the surface area of a piece of fret-work polishes much more quickly than do the larger flat surfaces.

Should the stain have been cut through accidentally in glass-papering, so that white edges have appeared, these must be carefully coloured before proceeding further. The rubber should then be recharged and a very small quantity of oil applied to its surface. It should then be applied to the flat surfaces with a circular motion which will produce smears (similar to those illustrated in Fig. 9) on the surface of the work. The smears will enable the operator to follow the progress of the rubber and to ensure that he covers the surface adequately. Commencing with a circular motion, up and down the surface of the work, as in Fig. 10, making about three or four sets of circular smears to an area equivalent to an average sideboard top, he can follow this with a figure-of-eight pattern, working across the grain (see Figs. 11 and 12). This may be followed by straight smears in line with the grain, as in Fig. 13. It should be his aim to vary both the size and shape of his smears, to secure an even deposit of polish over the whole surface and, by varying the direction of his approach, to force the polish into each individual grain.

With a growing thickness of polish on the surface of the work, there is a liability for a tackiness, which would cause the rubber to drag or stick to the surface, to develop. Linseed oil is therefore used as a lubricant, but it must be realised that it is the polish and not the oil which is responsible for the production of the final and permanent result and, although the oil itself may seem to increase the polish, the effect is evanescent and contributes nothing towards filling up the pores of the grain. Further, an excess of oil is inimical to the best work as it is a main contributory factor in the ultimate sweating of the work. The only sense in which oil can be said to hasten the operation is indirectly through its lubricating action, which enables the rubber to be applied more frequently and with more pressure than would otherwise be the case.

A newly charged rubber should be operated lightly at first and with gradually increasing pressure as it dries out. A rubber which has been worked too dry will tend to develop ropiness in the work, caused by the polish being insufficient to flow into the minute valleys and operating only on the higher portions. The secret, in successful French polishing, is chiefly a matter of leaving a suitable interval between successive applications of the rubber to allow the surface to dry sufficiently to lose its stickiness. This drying period tends to lengthen slightly as the work progresses but is essential if a fresh application of the rubber is to be made without the polish tearing up. This drying action is extremely superficial and must not be confused with hardening, which entails setting the work aside for some hours. While the surface is hardening, there is a considerable contraction of the polish as the spirit dries out, and those portions containing the greater depths of polish are inclined to be the most affected, so producing a slightly uneven surface. For this reason it is obvious that frequent hardening, although lengthening the process, is a valuable contributory factor towards delivering an ultimate finish which is both full and permanent.

There have been many methods adopted to hasten the bodying process and pumice powder is the material most frequently used. A little powdered pumice can be sprinkled on the surface of the work or, alternatively, applied to the rubber beneath its covering rag. In action, it has the tendency to grind the existing polish and to be deposited in the grain, the filling up of which it considerably hastens. It also has the effect, particularly when the rubber has been freshly charged, of acting rather harshly and tearing up the polish, so that care must be taken to avoid excessive working in the same place.

After several applications of polish, the pores will have become thoroughly filled. An experienced worker becomes aware of this by the smooth feeling of the rubber as it moves over the work, but the beginner will, perforce, rely upon visual evidence. The operator can now make some attempt to get rid of the oil smears. If the rubber has been worked out dry after each charging, all surplus oil will have been brought to the surface of the work, and a few applications of the rubber, in the direction of the grain, should obliterate any marks made in the circular motions. A few drops of methylated spirit on the face of the rubber will be a further help in eradicating the smears, but an excess of spirit should be avoided, as it may "burn" or roughen the surface and will tend to encourage the polish to sink into the wood. A final application of polish, free of oil, should produce a sensibly oil-free surface although, in fact, an oil smear or two at this stage is immaterial, as it will be dealt with in the succeeding stage.

The work must now be placed aside for at least a day, and longer if possible, to enable the spirit to dry out thoroughly from the depths of the polish. If the work has been hardened frequently throughout the bodying stage, an advantage will be obtained in the greater rapidity of the final hardening, and a reduced shrinkage of the polish into the grain.

The number of bodying operations which will be required is dependent upon the final finish desired and such variable factors as the quality of the polish, the type of the wood, and the thoroughness with which the groundwork has been prepared. Generally speaking, if a "piano" finish is required, two more bodying coats will be necessary before the finishing operation, but if it is to be "stiffed up" or "dulled down", one further coat should be sufficient.

Between each bodying operation, the work must be lightly glass-papered with worn No. oo glass-paper or with a beazer (see Fig. 3). In view of the time necessary to prepare a beazer, it is assumed that a beginner will be content, at least at first, to use glass-paper, but if considerable work is anticipated, it is well worth his while to make a beazer for future use.

A long strip of felt is soaked in linseed oil for a week and then liberally coated with powdered pumice. After being rolled up tightly into a cylinder, it should be firmly bound or sewn and hung up to dry and harden, a process which will take a few months to complete. It should then be cut across the middle, forming two pads, each with a perfectly flat surface. Used with a little oil and pumice, it will gently erase any slight ridges or nibs which may still be present on the work.

Before the finishing operation is started, the inside of the work should receive some attention, as a good interior finish adds considerably to the general appearance of the work. While on some occasions the interior is coloured to match the exterior, on others it is left in natural colour. In the latter case it should be bees-waxed and given a coat of button polish before being fadded up with a dry fad to produce an egg-shell polish. When the inside is to be treated uniformly in colour with the outside, it should originally have been stained rather lighter. It is then glass-papered and oiled with a mixture of one part white oil and one part paraffin oil, to which, if the work is of mahogany, dark oak, or walnut, some brown umber has been added. When the oil has dried thoroughly, the interior may, after a brush coating of button polish, be egg-shell polished with a fad. Book-cases should be treated similarly, but with the minimum use of oil, in order to avoid subsequent damage to the books. Cabinets with glazed doors should have the edges of exposed shelves polished to correspond with the exterior finish.

FINISHING

On this final operation depends the success or failure of the work. At this stage the article will be given characteristics anywhere between a hard, glittering, glass-like surface and a soft, semi-dulled smoothness, at the polisher's discretion. The surface should now be absolutely smooth and the chief defects at this moment will probably be slight traces of rubber marks and oil smears, and the inevitable small specks of dust that have settled on the surface during the hardening period. These can be removed by rubbing lightly with the beazer or, if this valuable adjunct has not been prepared, a moistened pad or soft brush dabbed in pumice powder.

Spiriting out.—Normally, work is finished by spiriting out and there are several variants of this operation, all of them producing a brilliant finish by burnishing the surface. Considerable care is necessary to prevent the methylated spirit from roughening, and so damaging, the polish and it is safer for the beginner to use the minimum amount of spirit and the rubber as lightly as possible.

When spiriting out the work by the first method, an ordinary polishing rubber is used, but it should first be cleaned with methylated spirit so as to rid it of any solidified polish or linseed oil, both of which may have congealed upon it in use. The rubber is then charged with a mixture of half polish and half spirit and worked out lightly and quickly on the surface of the work until dry. A very little oil is used and, towards the later stages, a little more methylated spirit should be added. The oil smear will now be somewhat thinner in appearance than in the bodying operation and it will be noticed that, as the rubber dries, the oil smear will become bluish in appearance. The application of a little spirit is made at this stage and will remove yet more of the oil and reveal a glass-like surface. To remove the final traces of oil another rubber, made up with flannel and moulded in the same way as the polishing rubber, should be charged with methylated spirit only and covered with a soft rag. Only practice and experience can indicate the degree of dampness which should be present. The beginner should err on the side of dryness and may find it an advantage to place this rubber in a special clean tin, or under an inverted can, for some hours, so that it tends to be drier externally and the action of the spirit less fierce on the surface. This rubber is known in the trade as a "ghost" and it is professional practice to test it for dampness on the bare arm or by application to the lips. The ghost should be applied to the work with a straight, sweeping movement, very lightly at first, but with a little pressure as it dries. At no time should the pressure be as heavy as when using the bodying rubber. The finished surface should now be free from flaws and traces of oil.

The second method of spiriting out is known as the "acid" finish and is preferred to the "ghost" by many polishers. Sulphuric acid (or vitriol) is used, but this varies considerably in strength and it is usual practice to dilute the acid with ten times the quantity of water. Care should be taken here and it should be remembered that water added to this acid produces great heat and may cause the sudden liberation of steam which can precipitate a mixture of acid and water into the face of the operator. For this reason, the acid should always be added to the water and never the water to the acid. Vienna chalk (not French chalk as is sometimes advised) should be placed in a loosely woven bag which can be dabbed lightly over the work and so distribute an even sprinkling of powder. A little of the acid solution should be poured into the clean palm of the hand and then rubbed with a circular motion or straight motion over the work. Sufficient solution and chalk should be used to form into a paste and the rubbing should be continued until the chalk dries off into a fine powder, when it may be dusted away. The acid has the effect of hardening the film of shellac and the chalk removes any oil from the surface of the work. Chamois leather may be used in preference to the palm of the hand for the final burnishing up.

A third method of spiriting out is by the use of grinding rubbers, but it is harder work and requires somewhat greater skill. The rubber is charged at the back with powdered pumice and covered with a coarse and open rag, not unlike fine white canvas. The pumice gradually seeps through the wadding and the canvas, the rubber becoming much harder than in the preceding methods and developing a greater pull on the work. The charging with polish and spirit is the same as before and must be followed by use of the ghost or, alternatively, vitriol and chalk. The results obtained in this way can be superior to those obtained by the other methods, expecially when performed by an experienced worker on the larger surfaces.

Stiffing up.—When the work is subsequently to be "stiffed up", the rubber is applied in the final bodying stages without oil and with straight movements in the direction of the grain, the addition of a little spirit on the face assisting materially in working the oil to the surface and in eradicating the rubber marks and smears. The stiffing-up process itself can be performed in either of two ways, known as the "dry stiff" and the "wet stiff" Experience will show the polisher with which of the two methods he can achieve the better results, but, whichever process is adopted, a piece of well-washed linen will be required.

If the dry method is being employed, the rubber should be lightly charged and moistened slightly with spirit to facilitate the easy flow of the polish from the wadding through the covering. It should then be worked out dry on the surface. The rubber should not be restricted to the straight motion unduly as, with a dry rubber, this may produce a ribby surface. In the final movements the rubber should be just damp and should pull on the surface and, providing it is working correctly, the operator should be able to hear a slight tearing or clicking sound on changing direction at the end of each stroke. The work when finished will present a dull satin-like surface which will dry to a bright finish in a few hours. As in most polishing operations, discretion must be used, as success often depends on knowing when to stop. This advice is equally applicable to stiffing in its wet form, in which operation the final rubber is well charged with polish and is applied in straight movements with the grain. Success, it must be reiterated, often depends on resisting the temptation to apply the rubber just once more.

Dulling down.—This finish is a variant of the stiffing-up process and produces a matt or semi-matt surface. It is commonly considered to give the work an appearance superior to any of the other methods and, in practice, most furniture—with the exception of pianos—is finished in this way. The result is particularly effective if the work has first been stiffed up with button polish by the dry method, as a surface will have been formed which will lend itself admirably to the dulling process. The effect is achieved by means of a soft-haired, flat-backed brush, similar to a boot brush, and fine emery powder or, failing this, some powdered pumice mixed with brown umber. The powder should be sprinkled on the face of the brush and applied to the surface of the work in a straight motion in the direction of the grain, the depth of the dulled finish being controllable by the amount of powder and the vigour of the brushing. When it is considered that sufficient dulling has been obtained, the work should be carefully wiped with a piece of rag and the corners and crevices cleaned out with a painter's fitch dipped in a mixture of paraffin and linseed oil, to which has been added a little brown umber, followed by careful wiping with a rag. A "dead dull" finish is obtained by first wiping over the surface of the work with a rag soaked in water and then applying the brush and powder as above. The water has a lubricating action which has the effect of enabling the abrasive to cut more keenly into the film of polish. Obviously, such operations should not be attempted with a surface that has not thoroughly hardened.

It is likely that, after the flat parts of the work have been finished, the mouldings will reveal a gloomy appearance, but a clean piece of wadding charged with "glaze" and covered with a piece of fine white velvet will produce a spirited-out effect. The glaze should be applied fairly wet, in a single application, and frets and other parts remaining patchy or dull may be similarly treated, a piece of wadding twisted round a match-stick being found quite suitable for very small work. Should the worker prefer, a china varnish can be used as an alternative to glaze for this purpose.

Chapter 3

Polishing Period Furniture

Period furniture falls definitely into one of two classes depending on whether the piece in question is appreciated for its artistry and craftsmanship or merely for its age. Accordingly, modern reproductions of period pieces are divisible between those stylized examples which, quite openly and frankly, exist as copies of what are admittedly fine examples of craftsmanship and design, and those in which such effects of time and wear and tear as fading or worm holes are introduced artificially, in a deliberate attempt to create a false impression of age. While the writer holds definitely to the view that the deliberate production of counterfeit work of this latter type is to be deplored, he, at the same time, realises that, from a purely technical angle, this work represents the highest level of the polisher's art and, for this reason alone, merits some attention in this manual.

It will probably be evident to the reader of the toregoing chapters, who, by now, will have some knowledge of polishing procedure, that the modern vogue of the flat surface and square edge materially simplifies the polisher's work. Equally, it will be appreciated that the intricacies of workmanship to be found, for instance, in articles by Chippendale or Sheraton will, by reason of their complexity and delicacy, call forth from the polisher a necessarily greater skill. The reader may also come to suspect that the almost universal craving for plainness in modern furniture has been inculcated in the general public as much to save manufacturing time as to conform to the virtues of "utility" and "simplicity".

Sheraton and Chippendale were cabinet makers who became famous by reason of the excellence of their work, executed with a superlative craftsmanship which has probably never been surpassed. While Chippendale worked almost exclusively in mahogany, Sheraton worked frequently also in satinwood. In view of the difference in treatment necessary they are dealt with here under separate headings.

SHERATON — MAHOGANY

The original Sheraton furniture, being made from the genuine Spanish mahogany, was initially of a rich colour which needed no reinforcement other than an application of red oil. It is very unlikely, however, that such timber will be available for any modern reproduction and some staining will, therefore, be necessary.

The most commonly used stain for this purpose is bichromate of potash: this should be dissolved in water and applied to the work with a swab of flannel or woollen cloth which has first been squeezed fairly dry. Some workers prefer to apply the stain with a brush, but it will generally be found more difficult to secure an even colour by this method.

The polisher must take care to use the staining solution at the correct strength. This can be found only by making a trial test on a piece of the same timber, which should first be cleaned up with a plane. Light has an appreciable influence on the colour achieved and both the test piece and the work itself should be allowed to dry naturally in full daylight after staining.

If, as is very likely, the article includes some ornamental banding or marquetry it is obvious that the stain must be prevented from destroying its colour effect. Protection is easily secured by carefully painting over such parts with white polish using a camel-hair pencil brush. Two applications should be made, great care being taken to cover the ornamentation completely while preventing any of the polish from encroaching on to the surrounding surface and thereby proofing that too, against the action of the stain. (It must also be remembered that a proofing of polish is only effective against a water-soluble stain and is of no effect should a spirit stain be substituted.)

Some adjustment in the concentration of the stain will need to be made before dealing with any edges exposing end grain since such portions, being relatively absorbent, tend to absorb the stain freely and, in consequence, to become much darker than the rest. Some workers control this by rubbing the end grain with a wax candle, but it is preferable, and also more reliable, to attain the correct colour by dilution of the stain itself.

When the solution has dried, it will be found that the bichromate has left a rust-like deposit on the surface which should be lightly glass-papered and dusted off, as otherwise it may produce a muddy or cloudy effect.

The polishing itself is carried out with orange polish which, in the bodying stage, is very slightly tinted with a drop or so of red stain made by dissolving Bismark brown in methylated spirit. This dye is extremely powerful and should be used with caution. It should be strained before use, only sufficient being added to the polish to colour it a very pale red.

After the bodying is completed the work is finished normally by spiriting out.

SHERATON — SATINWOOD

Satinwood pieces are normally polished throughout with white polish. This polish is manufactured from bleached shellac and, while not being strictly colourless, it affects the colour of the wood to which it is applied least of any of the polishes.

The filling-in operation, in so far as paste fillers and such substances are concerned, should be dispensed with and the grain choked from start to finish with rubbers of white polish.

The final finish will be obtained by spiriting out, except in the case of very small pieces where the process becomes impracticable. These are finished with a wet rubber well charged with glaze.

CHIPPENDALE — MAHOGANY

Genuine Chippendale furniture was polished to a dark red shade, but the original dyes have, with the passage of time, faded until the colour has now become brownish.

Several of the proprietary stains list a brown mahogany dye which forms the simplest way in which the effect can be attained. Alternatively, bichromate of potash staining followed by applications of brown polish will produce a similar effect. The polisher must guard against the work becoming too red, and neither red oil nor red polish should be used except possibly in the final bodying when the slightest trace may be used in order to remove the yellowish effect of the brown polish.

JACOBEAN OAK

There has recently been a considerable vogue for oak

furniture in a rather heavy style deemed to have been prevalent in earlier times. It has been given the name of "Jacobean" oak, but its artistic merit is doubtful and, strictly, it must be considered as fake antique, although, in the majority of instances, its age would deceive no-one. The polisher may, however, be required to finish an item of furniture made in this stylized "period" design, and details of staining and polishing are given here.

The significance of the Jacobean effect consists in the counterfeit impression of age attained by a system of staining which deliberately colours corners and crevices much darker than the rest of the work. The effect given is that of a piece of furniture which, over a long period, has been perfunctorily polished so that an accumulation of dirt, dust and polish has darkened the relatively inaccessible portions. In modern manufacture this effect must be obtained in the staining operation, and two stains are very suitable for this work.

The first is made by dissolving a quarter of a pound of asphaltum in one pint of turpentine to which is added, immediately before use, one ounce of gold size. The mixture should be strained before use and, after the work has thoroughly dried, it should be given a fastening coat of brush polish.

A rather better method is for the operator to stain the work with vandyke crystals dissolved in water, reducing the centres of panels and the tops of mouldings with a rag soaked in soda water. This operation should be performed with the rather casual action of a housewife wiping dust from a piece of furniture, the tendency being for the cloth to be effective on exposed portions and to miss corners, crevices and the depths of the mouldings and carvings. Care should be taken not to exaggerate the effect excessively and not to make too sharp a break between the lighter and darker areas, which should merge naturally. When the work has dried, it should be glass-papered carefully so as to avoid destroying the colouring. The whole work should now receive an application of wax polish which should be rubbed well into the grain and then thoroughly wiped off with a piece of coarse rag. The residue should be allowed to dry, and the whole work should then be stained with a medium oak oil stain applied with a piece of absorbent rag and afterwards wiped dry.

The oil stain will produce a pleasing effect more representative of a period piece than is usually secured, the wax preventing the open grain of the oak from absorbing an undue amount of the stain which would otherwise cause it to present an unpleasantly speckled appearance.

It is considered inappropriate to give work of this period a high polish or to polish it full grain and it should, therefore, be finished with wax polish or egg-shell polished with a French polish rubber.

LIMED OAK

The finish known as limed oak is secured by applying a paste composed of lime and water. This is well rubbed into the surface across the grain in the manner of a filler and then allowed to dry. The deposit is then brushed from the surface with a wire or stiff brush, leaving a filling of white lime in the indentations of the grain. The wood is finished in various colours according to requirements and taste, but it is usual to finish it with a greyish background which has the effect of throwing the liming into relief.

Should a background colour other than the natural

colour of the oak be required it will, of course, be obvious
that the necessary staining must be completed before the
lime is applied. Otherwise the white effect of the lime
in the grain will be destroyed.

FAKE ANTIQUE

Whatever the reader's beliefs in regard to the subject
of "faking", it will be obvious that, to be worth the effort
involved, the result should be capable of surviving
reasonable scrutiny without detection.

To achieve such a level of perfection will require very
considerable skill on the part of the polisher, coupled with
acute powers of observation. Before embarking on this
branch of his trade the polisher will be wise to examine
minutely all examples of genuine antique furniture that
he can discover.

The methods for simulating the various effects of wear
and tear are obvious enough, and they need only the
restraining influence of the polisher's discretion. Round-
ing the sharp edges of mouldings with fine glass-paper,
drilling tiny holes to represent worm tunnels, wire
brushing oak to give it a weather-beaten appearance and,
of course, deliberate denting and bruising of the wood,
are but a few of the commoner methods of "ageing" an
article. To these, a polisher of some originality will be
able to add many more.

The effects of time itself, as manifest primarily in the
fading brought about by strong sunlight, are more subtle
and need much observation and study on the part of the
polisher if the final result is to be convincing. Light
shades should be introduced both before and after staining by the use of oxalic acid, any necessary shading being
introduced during the bodying operations by means of a

mixture of lamp black, turpentine and gold size. An array of small bottles containing tinted polish of different colours will be most useful in securing the more subtle tones which will be required as the polisher's skill and ability increases.

Chapter 4

Preservation and Renovation

A periodical application of a wax furniture polish, accompanied by a vigorous rubbing with a duster, comprise the only form of protective treatment received by the majority of French polished articles of furniture in our homes. While this routine does both maintain and preserve the polished surface, it is deleterious in that too much is usually applied, with the consequent formation of a dust-collecting film. Dust, imprisoned beneath several layers of wax, each of which has contributed thereto its small quota, obscures the beauty of the original work and creates a muddy effect. It is, therefore, obviously essential, before endeavouring to protect or restore the polished surface of a piece of furniture, first to make sure that this surface is clean. Normally, it may be taken for granted that it is very far from being so, and warm water, a good, pure soap and a piece of muslin will be found to be surprisingly effective in removing all the dirt that has adhered since the previous treatment. The work can now be safely furbished with a very small amount of wax furniture polish and well rubbed so that only the minimum remains, as any heavy deposit of polish left on the work will tend to defeat the end in view by collecting a further deposit of dust.

Where the polished surface is showing signs of dullness or blooming, a polish reviver will do much to bring back its original lustre and brilliancy. In so far, however, as the polish reviver achieves its effects by partially redissolving the surface, it may be considered to be a polisher in reverse and, if used frequently or in excess, it will ultimately reduce the polish to such an extent that rebodying will become a necessity.

A recipe for making up a useful polish reviver is as follows:—

> 1 gill vinegar, 1 gill methylated spirit, ½ pint raw linseed oil, 1 oz. butter of antimony.

These ingredients should be placed in a bottle and well shaken before use and, according to some polishers, it is preferable to add a little Vienna chalk. A little of the polish reviver should be placed on a piece of wadding or soft rag, and applied to the work with a motion similar to that employed in bodying. The surface, after drying off, should be friction-polished with a warm, dry duster.

For the routine polishing of furniture after cleaning, an excellent wax polish consisting of bees-wax and turpentine can be made by shredding a cake of bees-wax into a stoppered jar of cold turpentine and periodically stirring with a stick until dissolved. Polishing wax made in this way takes about a day to prepare, but this time can be reduced by heating the turpentine. In view of the danger of fire, due to the inflammable nature of the turpentine, it is wise to restrict the heating to the placing of the turpentine in a vessel of hot water. As an alternative to bees-wax, which is rather expensive and not always obtainable, paraffin wax (as used in ordinary candle manufacture) may be substituted.

White stains on a French polished article can sometimes be removed if they are rubbed gently with cotton wool saturated in camphorated oil. Several applications may be necessary, which may result in a slight dulling of the polish.

The polisher may be confronted with an article which has been so misused or has received so many applications of polish reviver that repolishing has now become unavoidable. Here, he is on dangerous ground and, if expert advice is available, it should be obtained before the job is attempted. One difficulty will be his uncertainty as to the basis of the polish already on the article, the composition of which may make it necessary for him to modify his procedure in repolishing. To simplify the beginner's difficulty in coming to some decision as to the probable constitution of the polish where he has no access to an expert opinion, it may be useful to note some of the landmarks in the history of polishing as, in some instances, his difficulties can be resolved merely on a question of date.

From the innovation of French polish as a successor to the wax and oil polishing processes, up to the introduction of the mass-produced furniture of the machine age, it can be said that all polishing, in so far as it was performed by brush or rubber, was hand work, and invariably a solution of shellac, or some similar gum, in spirit was used. To reduce costs of production, in an endeavour to extend the furniture markets, it was essential that the very considerable time expended in hand polishing should be reduced. The first attempt at applying machinery to the polishing process was the normal one of mechanically reproducing, as closely as possible, the various manual operations of the polisher. Quite briefly, this machine consisted of an electric motor driving a revolving pad on a hollow spindle, through which French polish and methylated spirit could be fed to the rubber. Refinements were introduced to give the opera-

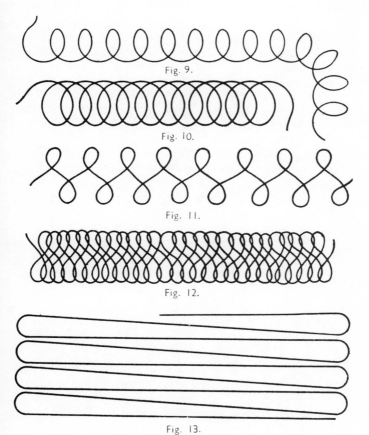

Fig. 9.

Fig. 10.

Fig. 11.

Fig. 12.

Fig. 13.

POLISHING MOVEMENTS

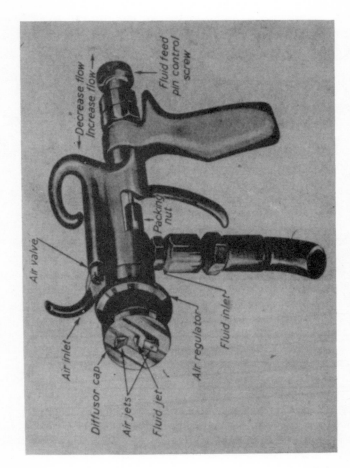

Decrease flow
Increase flow

Fluid feed pin control screw

Packing nut

Air valve

Air inlet

Diffusor cap

Air jets

Fluid jet

Air regulator

Fluid inlet

Fig. 14.—THE SPRAY GUN

tor some control but, due to the inherent difficulty of operating such a machine on anything other than a flat surface, and also possibly due to its unwieldiness and the cost of the plant, the power-driven rubber made little progress. The significant point to the renovator is, however, that an article polished by this means can, for his purpose, be treated as a hand-polished article, the constituents of the polish body being identical.

A method of applying polish by machinery, which is at once both more adaptable and more convenient for the large-scale manufacture of miscellaneous items of furniture, is afforded by the compressed air spraying plant. In this process the polish and colour are atomised and thrown on to the surface by compressed air. The result of this method is, in principle, little different from brush application, save that there is no dragging, unevenness of application, or brush marks with which to contend. Strictly, this process should fall under the heading of varnishing and, although the article may receive a finish chemically identical and superficially resembling hand polishing, it lacks the solid stability of the polish-filled grain and the soft lustre of its tone. Work executed by this process seems liable to chip, possibly through alteration in the constituents of the polish itself, and in general the article has a shorter span of usefulness. In some of the better-class articles, particularly those of mahogany and walnut, the use of the spray-gun is limited to the early varnishing stage, subsequent operations being performed by hand. This finish is not unsatisfactory, as the spray-gun, in this instance, has little more than replaced the normal application of brush polish, and the renovator will be quite safe in treating the work as hand polished.

A later development of polishing by spray-gun has resulted in the substitution of cellulose for the shellac polish. Here, although the work is not unattractive when new, it does not compare favourably with hand polishing from the point of view of quality.

The great disadvantage of a spray finish, whether of shellac or cellulose, is its superficiality; it does not penetrate into the pores of the wood. Successive applications do not intimately combine as in the hand method and the individual deposits, being so much thicker, engender a greater strain as a result of contraction when drying. The result is a pronounced tendency to crack and, where oil has been used in the primary processes, an increased possibility of the work sweating.

In renovating, therefore, the polisher must first of all come to some decision as to the category in which the original polish may be placed. If the work has originally been hand-polished or spray-cum-hand-polished, using shellac throughout, no particular difficulty should be encountered. The work should be washed down with warm water to which has been added some sugar soap or household soda. This should be only of sufficient strength to remove grease and dirt and any deposits of wax polish that may be on the surface. The work should then be rinsed with clean water and allowed to dry thoroughly. A coat of button polish applied with a brush will provide a good groundwork upon which to proceed with any filling, colouring or stopping, and after this, normal polishing procedure can be adopted.

The above is applicable only if the previous colour is to be perpetuated. If the work is to be darkened, the alteration can be achieved by colouring on top of the existing polish, but it is invariably better practice to strip the article down to bare wood before repolishing. The advantage of this latter method lies in the attainment of a transparent quality which would otherwise be unobtainable, and a similar procedure should be adopted if a lighter colour is required.

The polisher, in the course of his renovating work, will inevitably require to remove deposits of old polish. This may be achieved with the minimum of inconvenience by 'using two rags, one of which has been well soaked in methylated spirit. The spirit will gradually soften and dissolve the polish which may be wiped away with the second rag. Alternatively, there are some excellent spirituous paint strippers on the market which quickly remove old polish, but these are usually highly inflammable and of rather unpleasant odour. After using one of these stripping solutions, the work should be washed over with methylated spirit or soda water, according to the manufacturer's directions, to preclude the possibility of any residue having a deleterious effect upon the new polish.

After stripping down, the article may be treated exactly as new wood and the processes outlined in the previous chapters should be followed. In the case of work previously polished with cellulose, or in bad condition, the polisher will be safer to assume that stripping down to bare wood is a necessity. Methylated spirit will be ineffectual in this instance and he should obtain a special cellulose stripper.

In all cases, before proceeding with repolishing, the work must be well scraped down and glass-papered and, in the case of oak, which may have been darkened somewhat as a result of the stripper, it may be necessary first to bleach it with oxalic acid.

Chapter 5

Useful Hints

1.—The workshop should be kept clean and as free as possible from dust. Dust is one of the worst enemies of the French polisher. It clogs the rubber and settles on the work and generally contributes to the production of indifferent results.

2.—Do as much of your colouring and matching as possible in the first staining operation.

3.—Oil should never be used, except as part of the ingredients of a filler, until the colouring operation has been fastened with polish, or subsequent sweating may result. White oil is preferable to linseed oil and is particularly valuable in polishing natural-coloured work.

4.—Always recharge the rubber with the cover removed, although a spot of linseed oil or white oil may be added after the cover is in position.

5.—Use the minimum amount of lubricating oil consistent with the easy working of the rubber.

6.—If the covering has become gummy, move it to a cleaner part when recharging.

7.—Always keep the rubber moving and, if the polish roughens or drags, immediately set the work aside to harden. A little smoothing with glass-paper can then be attempted and the work carried on.

8.—Never hurry. Time plays a greater part in the achievement of the perfect polish than the distance covered by the rubber. A steady speed of approximately two strokes per second is all that is necessary.

9.—If the article is to be polished on both sides, care should be taken that one side is perfectly hard be ore placing it on the bench pads as, otherwise, it will be found impossible to remove the impression of the felt.

10.—Never leave your rubber on the bench all night, to become hard and unusable, but place it immediately in an air-tight tin.

11.—Brushes should never be left standing in the pot of colour or polish, as the ends of the hairs will bend and an even application of colour or polish will subsequently be found impossible. The brushes may be suspended without touching the bottom of the pot, by boring a small hole through the handle and slipping a piece of wire through, which will rest on both sides of the pot. Several brushes can be suspended from the same wire.

12.—At the end of a day's work, the colour or varnish should be strained from brushes by squeezing them between the lip of the bottle and the forefinger. The hairs should then be moulded to a point between the thumb and finger.

13. The operations of staining, filling and French polishing all discolour the hands. In general, it is useful to remember that the solvent used originally will also clean the hands. A rag soaked in methylated spirit will remove all traces of French polish, or varnish. Alternatively, household soda and hot water will be found quite effective. Bichromate of potash, turpentine and soda are the chief causative agents of dermatitis in the polishing trade. Rinsing the hands after washing, first in clean warm water and then in cold water, closes the pores and considerably reduces the risk.

14.—Glass-paper is most economically and conveniently used when a sheet is divided into six parts by dividing the long side into three and the shorter side in halves. It should always be used on a flat cork block.

15.—Much will be learnt if the beginner, instead of attempting at the outset to polish a large item of furniture, is content to apply the many processes outlined in this manual to a flat piece of wood, two square feet or so in area. The mastery of any small difficulties incurred during this trial run will be invaluable and will imbue him with the necessary confidence before embarking on larger and more intricate work.

Index

A

64   INDEX